MznLnx

Missing Links Exam Preps

Exam Prep for

Abstract Algebra

Herstein, 3rd Edition

The MznLnx Exam Prep is your link from the texbook and lecture to your exams.
The MznLnx Exam Preps are unauthorized and comprehensive reviews of your textbooks.

All material provided by MznLnx and Rico Publications (c) 2010
Textbook publishers and textbook authors do not particpate in or contribute to these reviews.

MznLnx

Rico
Publications

Exam Prep for Abstract Algebra
3rd Edition
Herstein

Publisher: Raymond Houge
Assistant Editor: Michael Rouger
Text and Cover Designer: Lisa Buckner
Marketing Manager: Sara Swagger
Project Manager, Editorial Production: Jerry Emerson
Art Director: Vernon Lowerui

Product Manager: Dave Mason
Editorial Asitant: Rachel Guzmanji
Pedagogy: Debra Long
Cover Image: Jim Reed/Getty Images
Text and Cover Printer: City Printing, Inc.
Compositor: Media Mix, Inc.

(c) 2010 Rico Publications
ALL RIGHTS RESERVED. No part of this work
covered by the copyright may be reproduced or
used in any form or by an means--graphic, electronic,
or mechanical, including photocopying, recording,
taping, Web distribution, information storage, and
retrieval systems, or in any other manner--without the
written permission of the publisher.

Printed in the United States
ISBN:

For more information about our products, contact us at:
Dave.Mason@RicoPublications.com

For permission to use material from this text or
product, submit a request online to:
Dave.Mason@RicoPublications.com

Contents

CHAPTER 1
Thins Familiar and Less Familiar — 1

CHAPTER 2
Groups — 10

CHAPTER 3
The Symmetric Group — 20

CHAPTER 4
Ring Theory — 22

CHAPTER 5
Fields — 33

CHAPTER 6
Special Topics (Optional) — 43

ANSWER KEY — 47

TO THE STUDENT

COMPREHENSIVE

The *MznLnx* Exam Prep series is designed to help you pass your exams. Editors at MznLnx review your textbooks and then prepare these practice exams to help you master the textbook material. Unlike study guides, workbooks, and practice tests provided by the texbook publisher and textbook authors, *MznLnx* gives you **all** of the material in each chapter in exam form, not just samples, so you can be sure to nail your exam.

MECHANICAL

The MznLnx Exam Prep series creates exams that will help you learn the subject matter as well as test you on your understanding. Each question is designed to help you master the concept. Just working through the exams, you gain an understanding of the subject--its a simple mechanical process that produces success.

INTEGRATED STUDY GUIDE AND REVIEW

MznLnx is not just a set of exams designed to test you, its also a comprehensive review of the subject content. Each exam question is also a review of the concept, making sure that you will get the answer correct without having to go to other sources of material. You learn as you go! Its the easiest way to pass an exam.

HUMOR

Studying can be tedious and dry. MznLnx's instructional design includes moderate humor within the exam questions on occassion, to break the tedium and revitalize the brain

Chapter 1. Thins Familiar and Less Familiar

1. In mathematics, a _____ is the direct product of two sets. The _____ is named after René Descartes, whose formulation of analytic geometry gave rise to this concept.

   Specifically, the _____ of two sets X (for example the points on an x-axis) and Y (for example the points on a y-axis), denoted X × Y, is the set of all possible ordered pairs whose first component is a member of X and whose second component is a member of Y (e.g. the whole of the x-y plane):

   $$X \times Y = \{(x,y) | x \in X \text{ and } y \in Y\}.$$

   For example, the _____ of the 13-element set of standard playing card ranks {Ace, King, Queen, Jack, 10, 9, 8, 7, 6, 5, 4, 3, 2} and the four-element set of card suits {â™ , â™¥, â™¦, â™£} is the 52-element set of all possible playing cards {(Ace, â™), (King, â™), ..., (2, â™), (Ace, â™¥), ..., (3, â™£), (2, â™£)}.

   a. -module
   b. -equivalence
   c. Pointed set
   d. Cartesian product

2. In mathematics, and more specifically set theory, the _____ is the unique set having no (zero) members. Some axiomatic set theories assure that the _____ exists by including an axiom of _____; in other theories, its existence can be deduced. Many possible properties of sets are trivially true for the _____.
   a. AKS primality test
   b. ADE classification
   c. Abelian P-root group
   d. Empty set

3. In mathematics, the _____ of two sets A and B is the set that contains all elements of A that also belong to B (or equivalently, all elements of B that also belong to A), but no other elements.

   For explanation of the symbols used in this article, refer to the table of mathematical symbols.

   The _____ of A and B

   The _____ of A and B is written 'A ∩ B'.

   a. ADE classification
   b. Abelian P-root group
   c. AKS primality test
   d. Intersection

Chapter 1. Thins Familiar and Less Familiar

4. In set theory, the term _____ refers to a set operation used in the convergence of set elements to form a resultant set containing the elements of both sets. As a simple example, a _____ of two disjoint sets, which do not have elements in common results in a set containing all elements from both sets. A Venn diagram representing the _____ of sets A and B. If one circle represents A, and the other B, then the red area represents the _____ of A and B. The area where the circles join, also shown in red, is the intersection of the two sets.

If we define two sets which contain unique elements; those of A not occurring in B and vice versa, then the _____ of these sets results in a set which contains all elements of A and B. In terms of notation, we could define this set operation as the following:

A = {1,2,3,4}
B = {5,6,7,8}
$$A \cup B = \{1, 2, 3, 4, 5, 6, 7, 8\}$$

Other more complex operations can be done including the _____, if the set is for example defined by a property rather than a finite or assumed infinite enumeration of elements.

a. AKS primality test
b. Union
c. Abelian P-root group
d. ADE classification

5. In discrete mathematics and predominantly in set theory, a _____ is a concept used in comparisons of sets to refer to the unique values of one set in relation to another. The terms 'absolute' and 'relative' _____ refer to more specific applications of the concept, with universal _____s referring to elements unique to the universal set and the latter referring to the unique elements of one set in relation to another. In this image, the universal set is represented by the border of the image, and the set A as a disc.

a. Pointed set
b. -module
c. Complement
d. -equivalence

6. In linear algebra and functional analysis, a _____ is a linear transformation P from a vector space to itself such that $P^2 = P$. It leaves its image unchanged. Though abstract, this definition of '_____' formalizes and generalizes the idea of graphical _____.

a. Convolution power
b. C_0-semigroup
c. Lumer-Phillips theorem
d. Projection

7. Formally, a binary operation ∗ on a set S is called associative if it satisfies the _____:

$$(x * y) * z = x * (y * z) \quad \text{for all } x, y, z \in S.$$
Using * to denote a binary operation performed on a set

$$(xy)z = x(yz) = xyz \quad \text{for all } x, y, z \in S.$$
An example of multiplicative associativity

The evaluation order does not affect the value of such expressions, and it can be shown that the same holds for expressions containing any number of ∗ operations. Thus, when ∗ is associative, the evaluation order can therefore be left unspecified without causing ambiguity, by omitting the parentheses and writing simply:

xyz,

However, it is important to remember that changing the order of operations does not involve or permit changing the actual operations themselves by moving the operands around within the expression.

A very different perspective is obtained by rephrasing associativity using functional notation: f(f(x,y),z) = f(x,f(y,z)): when expressed in this form, associativity becomes less obvious.

a. Abelian P-root group
b. ADE classification
c. AKS primality test
d. Associative law

8. A _____ is a set G closed under a binary operation · satisfying the following 3 axioms:

- Associativity: For all a, b and c in G, (a · b) · c = a · (b · c.)
- Identity element: There exists an e∈G such that for all a in G, e · a = a · e = a.
- Inverse element: For each a in G, there is an element b in G such that a · b = b · a = e, where e is an identity element.

Basic examples for _____s are the integers Z with addition operation, or rational numbers without zero Q{0} with multiplication. More generally, for any ring R, the units in R form a multiplicative _____ Groups include, however, much more general structures than the above.

a. Group
b. Nilpotent group
c. Product of group subsets
d. Grigorchuk group

Chapter 1. Thins Familiar and Less Familiar

9. The _____ are natural numbers including 0 ' href='/wiki/0_(number)'>0, 1, 2, 3, ...) and their negatives (0, −1, −2, −3, ...). They are numbers that can be written without a fractional or decimal component, and fall within the set {...

   a. Abelian P-root group
   b. AKS primality test
   c. Integers
   d. ADE classification

10. In algebraic geometry, _____s are a generalization of codimension one subvarieties of algebraic varieties; two different generalizations are in common use, Cartier _____s and Weil _____s The concepts agree on non-singular varieties over algebraically closed fields.

    A Weil _____ is a locally finite linear combination (with integral coefficients) of irreducible subvarieties of codimension one.

    a. Linear system of divisors
    b. Lefschetz pencil
    c. Picard group
    d. Divisor

11. Informally, the _____ of two polynomials p(x) and q(x) is the 'biggest' polynomial that divides evenly into both p(x) and q(x.) The definition is modeled on the concept of the _____ of two integers. This is simply the greatest integer that divides into both of them with a remainder of zero.

    a. Descartes' rule of signs
    b. Coefficient
    c. Ring of symmetric functions
    d. Greatest common divisor

12. In mathematics, the _____s are an extension of the real numbers obtained by adjoining an imaginary unit, denoted i, which satisfies:

$$i^2 = -1.$$

Every _____ can be written in the form a + bi, where a and b are real numbers called the real part and the imaginary part of the _____, respectively.

_____s are a field, and thus have addition, subtraction, multiplication, and division operations. These operations extend the corresponding operations on real numbers, although with a number of additional elegant and useful properties, e.g., negative real numbers can be obtained by squaring complex (imaginary) numbers.

a. -equivalence
b. Complex number
c. -module
d. 2-bridge knot

13. In algebra, a _____ of an element in a quadratic extension field of a field K is its image under the unique non-identity automorphism of the extended field that fixes K. If the extension is generated by a square root of an element r of K, then the _____ of $a + b\sqrt{r}$ is $a - b\sqrt{r}$ for $a, b \in K$, and in particular in the case of the field C of complex numbers as an extension of the field R of real numbers (where r = − 1), the complex _____ of a + bi is a − bi.

Forming the sum or product of any element of the extension field with its _____ always gives an element of K. This can be used to rewrite a quotient of numbers in the extended field so that the denominator lies in K, by multiplying numerator and denominator by the _____ of the denominator. This process is called rationalization of the denominator, in particular if K is the field Q of rational numbers.

a. Digital root
b. K-theory
c. Conjugate
d. Field arithmetic

14. In mathematics, in particular field theory, the _____ of an algebraic element α, over a field K, are the (other) roots of the minimal polynomial

$P_{K,\alpha}(t)$

of α over K.

For example, the cube roots of the number one are:

$$\sqrt[3]{1} = \begin{cases} 1 \\ -\frac{1}{2} + \frac{\sqrt{3}}{2}i \\ -\frac{1}{2} - \frac{\sqrt{3}}{2}i \end{cases}$$

The latter two roots are _____ in the field K = Q[√−3].

If K is given inside an algebraically closed field C, then the conjugates can be taken inside C. Usually one includes α itself in the set of conjugates.

Chapter 1. Thins Familiar and Less Familiar

a. Primitive polynomial
b. Field extension
c. Totally real
d. Conjugate elements

15. In mathematics, the (formal) _____ of a complex vector space V is the complex vector space $\overline{V}$ consisting of all formal _____s of elements of V. That is, $\overline{V}$ is a vector space whose elements are in one-to-one correspondence with the elements of V:

$$\overline{V} = \{\overline{v} \mid v \in V\},$$

with the following rules for addition and scalar multiplication:

$$\overline{v} + \overline{w} = \overline{v+w} \quad \text{and} \quad \alpha\overline{v} = \overline{\overline{\alpha}\,v}.$$

Here v and w are vectors in V, α is a complex number, and $\overline{\alpha}$ denotes the _____ of α.

In the case where V is a linear subspace of $\mathbb{C}^n$, the formal _____ $\overline{V}$ is naturally isomorphic to the actual _____ subspace of V in $\mathbb{C}^n$.

a. Conjugate transpose
b. Polynomial basis
c. Complex conjugate
d. Binomial inverse theorem

16. In mathematics, an _____ is a complex number whose squared value is a real number less than or equal to zero. The imaginary unit, denoted by i or j, is an example of an _____. If y is a real number, then iÂ·y is an _____, because:

$$(i \cdot y)^2 = i^2 \cdot y^2 = -y^2 \leq 0.$$

_____s were defined in 1572 by Rafael Bombelli.

a. Abelian P-root group
b. ADE classification
c. Imaginary Number
d. AKS primality test

17. In mathematics, an _____ is a statement about the relative size or order of two objects, or about whether they are the same or not

- The notation a < b means that a is less than b.
- The notation a > b means that a is greater than b.
- The notation a ≠ b means that a is not equal to b, but does not say that one is bigger than the other or even that they can be compared in size.

In all these cases, a is not equal to b, hence, '_____'.

These relations are known as strict _____

- The notation a ≤ b means that a is less than or equal to b (or, equivalently, not greater than b);
- The notation a ≥ b means that a is greater than or equal to b (or, equivalently, not smaller than b);

An additional use of the notation is to show that one quantity is much greater than another, normally by several orders of magnitude.

- The notation a ≪ b means that a is much less than b.
- The notation a ≫ b means that a is much greater than b.

If the sense of the _____ is the same for all values of the variables for which its members are defined, then the _____ is called an 'absolute' or 'unconditional' _____. If the sense of an _____ holds only for certain values of the variables involved, but is reversed or destroyed for other values of the variables, it is called a conditional _____.

One can apply the same algebraic operations to inequalities as one would apply for solving equalities. For example, to find x for the _____ 10x > 20 one would divide 20 by 10 to obtain x > 2.

a. AKS primality test
b. Abelian P-root group
c. ADE classification
d. Inequality

18. A _____ is one of the basic shapes of geometry: a polygon with three corners or vertices and three sides or edges which are line segments. A _____ with vertices A, B, and C is denoted ABC.

In Euclidean geometry any three non-collinear points determine a unique _____ and a unique plane (i.e. a two-dimensional Euclidean space.)

a. -equivalence
  b. 2-bridge knot
  c. -module
  d. Triangle

19. In mathematics, the _____ states that for any triangle, the length of a given side must be less than the sum of the other two sides but greater than the difference between the two sides.

In Euclidean geometry and some other geometries this is a theorem. In the Euclidean case, in both the less than or equal to and greater than or equal to statements, equality occurs only if the triangle has a 180° angle and two 0° angles, as shown in the bottom example in the image to the right.

  a. 2-bridge knot
  b. -module
  c. -equivalence
  d. Triangle Inequality

20. In mathematics, the _____ of a real number is its numerical value without regard to its sign. So, for example, 3 is the _____ of both 3 and −3.

The _____ of a number a is denoted by $|a|$.

  a. Abelian P-root group
  b. AKS primality test
  c. Absolute value
  d. ADE classification

21. In mathematics, a _____ of a number x is any number which, when repeatedly multiplied by itself, eventually yields x:

$$r \times r \times \cdots \times r = x.$$

In terms of exponentiation, r is a _____ of x if

$$r^n = x$$

for some positive integer n. For example, 2 is a _____ of 16 since $2^4 = 2 \times 2 \times 2 \times 2 = 16$.

The number n is called the degree of the _____.

a. Cubic function
b. Rationalisation
c. Difference of two squares
d. Root

22. An nth _____, where n = 1,2,3,···, is a complex number, z, satisfying the equation

$$z^n = 1.$$

Second roots are called square roots, and third roots are called cube roots.

An nth _____ is primitive if

$$z^k \neq 1 \quad (k = 1, 2, 3, \ldots, n-1).$$

There are n different nth roots of unity:

$$z^k \quad (k = 1, 2, 3, \ldots, n),$$

where z is any primitive nth _____. These n roots are distributed evenly over the unit circle as can be seen in the plot on the right-hand side of the three 3rd roots of unity.

a. 2-bridge knot
b. Root of unity
c. -equivalence
d. -module

Chapter 2. Groups

1. In mathematics, an _____ is a special type of element of a set with respect to a binary operation on that set. It leaves other elements unchanged when combined with them. This is used for groups and related concepts.

    a. Isomorphism class
    b. Orthogonal
    c. Algebraic K-theory
    d. Identity element

2. In mathematics, a _____ in a (unital) ring R is an invertible element of R, i.e. an element u such that there is a v in R with

   $uv = vu = 1_R$, where 1_R is the multiplicative identity element.

   That is, u is an invertible element of the multiplicative monoid of R. If $0 \neq 1$ in the ring, then 0 is not a _____.

   Unfortunately, the term _____ is also used to refer to the identity element 1_R of the ring, in expressions like ring with a _____ or _____ ring, and also e.g. '_____' matrix.

    a. Ascending chain condition on principal ideals
    b. Ore condition
    c. Ore extension
    d. Unit

3. A _____ is a set G closed under a binary operation · satisfying the following 3 axioms:

   - Associativity: For all a, b and c in G, (a · b) · c = a · (b · c.)
   - Identity element: There exists an e∈G such that for all a in G, e · a = a · e = a.
   - Inverse element: For each a in G, there is an element b in G such that a · b = b · a = e, where e is an identity element.

   Basic examples for _____s are the integers Z with addition operation, or rational numbers without zero Q{0} with multiplication. More generally, for any ring R, the units in R form a multiplicative _____ Groups include, however, much more general structures than the above.

    a. Group
    b. Grigorchuk group
    c. Product of group subsets
    d. Nilpotent group

Chapter 2. Groups

4. In group theory, a branch of mathematics, the term _____ is used in two closely related senses:

   - the _____ of a group is its cardinality, i.e. the number of its elements;
   - the _____, sometimes period, of an element a of a group is the smallest positive integer m such that a^m = e (where e denotes the identity element of the group, and a^m denotes the product of m copies of a.) If no such m exists, we say that a has infinite _____. All elements of finite groups have finite _____.

We denote the _____ of a group G by ord(G) or $|G|$ and the _____ of an element a by ord(a) or $|a|$.

Example. The symmetric group S_3 has the following multiplication table.

This group has six elements, so ord(S_3) = 6.

   a. Artin group
   b. Outer automorphism group
   c. Index calculus algorithm
   d. Order

5. In mathematics, a _____ of a number x is any number which, when repeatedly multiplied by itself, eventually yields x:

$$r \times r \times \cdots \times r = x.$$

In terms of exponentiation, r is a _____ of x if

$$r^n = x$$

for some positive integer n. For example, 2 is a _____ of 16 since 2^4 = 2 × 2 × 2 × 2 = 16.

The number n is called the degree of the _____.

   a. Root
   b. Rationalisation
   c. Cubic function
   d. Difference of two squares

6. An _____ is a group satisfying the requirement that the result of applying the group operation to two group elements does not depend on their order _____s generalize the arithmetic of addition of integers; they are named after Niels Henrik Abel.

Chapter 2. Groups

The concept of an _____ is one of the first concepts encountered in undergraduate abstract algebra, with many other basic objects, such as a module and a vector space, being its refinements.

a. Elementary abelian group
b. Algebraically compact
c. ADE classification
d. Abelian group

7. The term _____ or centre is used in various contexts in abstract algebra to denote the set of all those elements that commute with all other elements. More specifically:

- The _____ of a group G consists of all those elements x in G such that xg = gx for all g in G. This is a normal subgroup of G.
- The _____ of a ring R is the subset of R consisting of all those elements x of R such that xr = rx for all r in R. The _____ is a commutative subring of R, so R is an algebra over its _____.
- The _____ of an algebra A consists of all those elements x of A such that xa = ax for all a in A. See also: central simple algebra.
- The _____ of a Lie algebra L consists of all those elements x in L such that [x,a] = 0 for all a in L. This is an ideal of the Lie algebra L.
- The _____ of a monoidal category C consists of pairs (A,u) where A is an object of C, and $u : A \otimes - \to - \otimes A$ a natural isomorphism satisfying certain axioms.

a. Left alternative
b. Ring theory
c. Self-adjoint
d. Center

8. In group theory, a _____ is a group that can be generated by a single element, in the sense that the group has an element g (called a 'generator' of the group) such that, when written multiplicatively, every element of the group is a power of g (a multiple of g when the notation is additive.) The 6th complex roots of unity form a _____ under multiplication. ζ is a primitive element, but ζ^2 is not, because the odd powers of ζ are not a power of ζ^2.

A group G is called cyclic if there exists an element g in G such that G = <g> = { g^n | n is an integer }.

a. Locally cyclic group
b. Torsion subgroup
c. Finitely generated abelian group
d. Cyclic group

Chapter 2. Groups

9. In mathematics and especially in abstract algebra, a _____ or simply congruence is an equivalence relation that is compatible with some algebraic operation(s.)

The prototypical example is modular arithmetic: for n a positive integer, two integers a and b are called congruent modulo n if a − b is divisible by n (or an equivalent condition is that they give the same remainder when divided by n.)

For example, 5 and 11 are congruent modulo 3:

$$11 \equiv 5 \pmod{3}$$

because 11 − 5 gives 6, which is divisible by 3.

 a. Congruence relation
 b. Modular arithmetic
 c. Multiplicative group of integers modulo n
 d. Discrete logarithm

10. In algebra, a _____ of an element in a quadratic extension field of a field K is its image under the unique non-identity automorphism of the extended field that fixes K. If the extension is generated by a square root of an element r of K, then the _____ of $a + b\sqrt{r}$ is $a - b\sqrt{r}$ for $a, b \in K$, and in particular in the case of the field C of complex numbers as an extension of the field R of real numbers (where r = − 1), the complex _____ of a + bi is a − bi.

Forming the sum or product of any element of the extension field with its _____ always gives an element of K. This can be used to rewrite a quotient of numbers in the extended field so that the denominator lies in K, by multiplying numerator and denominator by the _____ of the denominator. This process is called rationalization of the denominator, in particular if K is the field Q of rational numbers.

 a. Digital root
 b. Conjugate
 c. K-theory
 d. Field arithmetic

11. In mathematics, in particular field theory, the _____ of an algebraic element α, over a field K, are the (other) roots of the minimal polynomial

$$P_{K,\alpha}(t)$$

of α over K.

For example, the cube roots of the number one are:

$$\sqrt[3]{1} = \begin{cases} 1 \\ -\frac{1}{2} + \frac{\sqrt{3}}{2}i \\ -\frac{1}{2} - \frac{\sqrt{3}}{2}i \end{cases}$$

The latter two roots are _____ in the field K = Q[√−3].

If K is given inside an algebraically closed field C, then the conjugates can be taken inside C. Usually one includes α itself in the set of conjugates.

a. Totally real
b. Field extension
c. Primitive polynomial
d. Conjugate elements

12. A _____ is a left or right _____ of some subgroup in G. Since Hg = g(g⁻¹Hg), the right _____s Hg (of H) and the left _____s g(g⁻¹Hg) (of the conjugate subgroup g⁻¹Hg) are the same. Hence it is not meaningful to speak of a _____ as being left or right unless one first specifies the underlying subgroup.

For abelian groups or groups written additively, the notation used changes to g+H and H+g respectively.

a. Grigorchuk group
b. Burnside ring
c. Coset
d. Wreath product

13. In mathematics, specifically group theory, the _____ of a subgroup H in a group G is the e;relative sizee; of H in G. For example, if H has _____ 2 in G, then intuitively e;halfe; of the elements of G lie in H. The _____ of H in G is usually denoted |G : H| or [G : H].

If G and H are finite groups, then the _____ of H in G is simply the quotient of the orders of the two groups:

$$|G : H| = \frac{|G|}{|H|}.$$

By Lagrange's theorem, this number is always a positive integer.

If G and H are infinite, then the _____ of H is G is defined as the number of cosets of H in G.

a. Outer automorphism
b. Even permutations
c. Inner automorphism
d. Index

14. In mathematics, more specifically in abstract algebra, a _____ is a special kind of subgroup. _____s are important because they can be used to construct quotient groups from a given group.

Évariste Galois was the first to realize the importance of the existence of _____s.

a. Hanna Neumann conjecture
b. Characteristic subgroup
c. Cayley graph
d. Normal subgroup

15. A _____ between two algebras over a field K, A and B, is a map $F : A \to B$ such that for all k in K and x,y in A,

- $F(kx) = kF(x)$

- $F(x + y) = F(x) + F(y)$

- $F(xy) = F(x)F(y)$

If F is bijective then F is said to be an isomorphism between A and B.

Let A = K[x] be the set of all polynomials over a field K and B be the set of all polynomial functions over K. Both A and B are algebras over K given by the standard multiplication and addition of polynomials and functions, respectively. We can map each f in A to $\hat{f}$ in B by the rule $\hat{f}(t) = f(t)$. A routine check shows that the mapping $f \mapsto \hat{f}$ is a _____ of the algebras A and B. If K is a finite field then let

$$p(x) = \Pi_{t \in K}(x - t).$$

p is a nonzero polynomial in K[x], however $p(t) = 0$ for all t in K, so $\hat{p} = 0$ is the zero function and the algebras are not isomorphic.

a. Tensor algebra
b. Tensor product of algebras
c. Frobenius matrix
d. Homomorphism

16. In mathematics, an _____ is an isomorphism from a mathematical object to itself. It is, in some sense, a symmetry of the object, and a way of mapping the object to itself while preserving all of its structure. The set of all _____s of an object forms a group, called the _____ group.
   a. Epimorphism
   b. Endomorphism
   c. ADE classification
   d. Automorphism

17. In abstract algebra, an _____ is a bijective map f such that both f and its inverse f^{-1} are homomorphisms, i.e., structure-preserving mappings. In the more general setting of category theory, an _____ is a morphism f:X→Y in a category for which there exists an 'inverse' f^{-1}:Y→X, with the property that both $f^{-1}f=id_X$ and $ff^{-1}=id_Y$.

Informally, an _____ is a kind of mapping between objects, which shows a relationship between two properties or operations.

   a. Endomorphism
   b. ADE classification
   c. Epimorphism
   d. Isomorphism

18. In the context of abstract algebra or universal algebra, a _____ is an injective homomorphism. A _____ from X to Y is often denoted with the notation $X \hookrightarrow Y$.

In the more general setting of category theory, a _____ is a left-cancellative morphism, that is, a map f : X → Y such that, for all morphisms $g_1, g_2 : Z \to X$,

$$f \circ g_1 = f \circ g_2 \Rightarrow g_1 = g_2.$$

_____s are a categorical generalization of injective functions; in some categories the notions coincide, but _____s are more general, as in the examples below.

a. 2-bridge knot
b. -module
c. Monomorphism
d. -equivalence

19. In abstract algebra, an _____ of a group G is a function

$$f : G \to G$$

defined by

$$f(x) = axa^{-1}, \text{ for all } x \text{ in } G,$$

where a is a given fixed element of G.

The operation axa^{-1} is called conjugation Informally, in a conjugation a certain operation is applied, then another one (x) is carried out, and then the initial operation is reversed.

a. Inner Automorphism
b. Idempotent measure
c. Extensible automorphism
d. IA automorphism

20. In the various branches of mathematics that fall under the heading of abstract algebra, the _____ of a homomorphism measures the degree to which the homomorphism fails to be injective. An important special case is the _____ of a matrix, also called the null space.

The definition of _____ takes various forms in various contexts.

a. Completing the square
b. K-theory
c. Monomial basis
d. Kernel

21. In group theory, a Dedekind group is a group G such that every subgroup of G is normal. All abelian groups are Dedekind groups. A non-abelian Dedekind group is called a _____.

Chapter 2. Groups

   a. Schreier conjecture
   b. Frobenius theorem
   c. Dixmier conjecture
   d. Hamiltonian group

22. In mathematics, the _____ of a ring R, often denoted char(R), is defined to be the smallest number of times one must add the ring's multiplicative identity element (1) to itself to get the additive identity element (0); the ring is said to have _____ zero if this repeated sum never reaches the additive identity. That is, char(R) is the smallest positive number n such that

$$\underbrace{1 + \cdots + 1}_{n \text{ summands}} = 0$$

if such a number n exists, and 0 otherwise. The _____ may also be taken to be the exponent of the ring's additive group, that is, the smallest positive n such that

$$\underbrace{a + \cdots + a}_{n \text{ summands}} = 0$$

for every element a of the ring (again, if n exists; otherwise zero.)

   a. Free ideal ring
   b. Characteristic
   c. Coherent ring
   d. Hereditary

23. In mathematics, particularly in the area of abstract algebra known as group theory, a _____ is a subgroup that is invariant under all automorphisms of the parent group. Because conjugation is an automorphism, every _____ is normal, though not every normal subgroup is characteristic. Examples of _____s include the commutator subgroup and the center of a group.
   a. Composition series
   b. Principal homogeneous space
   c. Group object
   d. Characteristic subgroup

24. In mathematics, one can often define a _____ of objects already known, giving a new one. This is generally the Cartesian product of the underlying sets, together with a suitably defined structure on the product set. More abstractly, one talks about the product in category theory, which formalizes these notions.

a. Precedence rule
b. Direct product
c. Special linear group
d. Group extension

25. The _____ are natural numbers including 0 ' href='/wiki/0_(number)'>0, 1, 2, 3, ...) and their negatives (0, −1, −2, −3, ...). They are numbers that can be written without a fractional or decimal component, and fall within the set {...
   a. AKS primality test
   b. Abelian P-root group
   c. ADE classification
   d. Integers

Chapter 3. The Symmetric Group

1. In mathematics, and in particular in group theory, a _____ is a permutation of the elements of some set X which maps the elements of some subset S to each other in a cyclic fashion, while fixing (i.e., mapping to themselves) all other elements. The set S is called the orbit of the _____.

A permutation of a set X, which is a bijective function $\sigma : X \to X$, is called a _____ if the action on X of the subgroup generated by σ has exactly one orbit with more than a single element.

   a. Definition .
   b. Cycle
   c. Continuant
   d. Nested radical

2. In several fields of mathematics the term _____ is used with different but closely related meanings. They all relate to the notion of mapping the elements of a set to other elements of the same set, i.e., exchanging (or 'permuting') elements of a set.

The general concept of _____ can be defined more formally in different contexts:

In combinatorics, a _____ is usually understood to be a sequence containing each element from a finite set once, and only once.

   a. Binary function
   b. Rupture field
   c. Near-field
   d. Permutation

3. A _____ is a set G closed under a binary operation · satisfying the following 3 axioms:

   - Associativity: For all a, b and c in G, (a · b) · c = a · (b · c.)
   - Identity element: There exists an e∈G such that for all a in G, e · a = a · e = a.
   - Inverse element: For each a in G, there is an element b in G such that a · b = b · a = e, where e is an identity element.

Basic examples for _____s are the integers Z with addition operation, or rational numbers without zero Q{0} with multiplication. More generally, for any ring R, the units in R form a multiplicative _____ Groups include, however, much more general structures than the above.

   a. Group
   b. Grigorchuk group
   c. Product of group subsets
   d. Nilpotent group

Chapter 3. The Symmetric Group

4. In mathematics, an _____ is the group of even permutations of a finite set. The _____ on the set {1,...,n} is called the _____ of degree n, or the _____ on n letters and denoted by A_n or Alt(n.)

For instance, the _____ of degree 4 is A_4 = {e, (123), (132), (124), (142), (134), (143), (234), (243), (12)(34), (13)(24), (14)(23)}

a. Alternating group
b. Octahedral symmetry
c. Icosahedral symmetry
d. Extra special groups

5. In mathematics, the term _____ is used to describe an algebraic structures which in some sense cannot be divided by a smaller structure of the same type. Put another way, an algebraic structure is _____ if the kernel of every homomorphism is either the whole structure or a single element. Some examples are:

- A group is called a _____ group if it does not contain a non-trivial proper normal subgroup.
- A ring is called a _____ ring if it does not contain a non-trivial two sided ideal.
- A module is called a _____ module if does not contain a non-trivial submodule.
- An algebra is called a _____ algebra if does not contain a non-trivial two sided ideal.

The general pattern is that the structure admits no non-trivial congruence relations.

a. Polarization identity
b. Commutativity
c. Linear combinations
d. Simple

Chapter 4. Ring Theory

1. In mathematics, a _____ is a type of algebraic structure. There is some variation among mathematicians as to exactly what properties a _____ is required to have, as described in detail below. However, commonly a _____ is defined as a set together with two binary operations (usually called addition and multiplication), where each operation combines two elements to form a third element.

    a. 2-bridge knot
    b. Ring
    c. -equivalence
    d. -module

2. In mathematics, a _____ in a (unital) ring R is an invertible element of R, i.e. an element u such that there is a v in R with

    $uv = vu = 1_R$, where 1_R is the multiplicative identity element.

    That is, u is an invertible element of the multiplicative monoid of R. If $0 \neq 1$ in the ring, then 0 is not a _____.

    Unfortunately, the term _____ is also used to refer to the identity element 1_R of the ring, in expressions like ring with a _____ or _____ ring, and also e.g. '_____' matrix.

    a. Ore condition
    b. Ascending chain condition on principal ideals
    c. Unit
    d. Ore extension

3. A _____ is a set G closed under a binary operation · satisfying the following 3 axioms:

    - Associativity: For all a, b and c in G, (a · b) · c = a · (b · c.)
    - Identity element: There exists an e∈G such that for all a in G, e · a = a · e = a.
    - Inverse element: For each a in G, there is an element b in G such that a · b = b · a = e, where e is an identity element.

    Basic examples for _____s are the integers Z with addition operation, or rational numbers without zero Q{0} with multiplication. More generally, for any ring R, the units in R form a multiplicative _____ Groups include, however, much more general structures than the above.

    a. Grigorchuk group
    b. Nilpotent group
    c. Product of group subsets
    d. Group

4. In ring theory, a branch of abstract algebra, a _____ is a ring in which the multiplication operation is commutative. The study of _____s is called commutative algebra.

Some specific kinds of _____s are given with the following chain of class inclusions:

- _____s ⊃ integral domains ⊃ unique factorization domains ⊃ principal ideal domains ⊃ Euclidean domains ⊃ fields

A ring is a set R equipped with two binary operations, i.e. operations that combine any two elements of the ring to a third. They are called addition and multiplication and commonly denoted by '+' and '·', e.g. a + b and a · b.

a. Going up
b. Nilradical
c. Differential calculus over commutative algebras
d. Commutative ring

5. In mathematics, especially in elementary arithmetic, _____ is an arithmetic operation which is the inverse of multiplication.

Specifically, if c times b equals a, written:

$$c \times b = a$$

where b is not zero, then a divided by b equals c, written:

$$\frac{a}{b} = c$$

For instance,

$$\frac{6}{3} = 2$$

since

$$2 \times 3 = 6.$$

In the above expression, a is called the dividend, b the divisor and c the quotient.

Chapter 4. Ring Theory

a. -module
b. Division
c. 2-bridge knot
d. -equivalence

6. In abstract algebra, a _____ is a ring in which division is possible. More formally, a ring with 0 ≠ 1 is a _____ if every non-zero element a has a multiplicative inverse _____s differ from fields only in that their multiplication is not required to be commutative.
   a. Division ring
   b. Local ring
   c. Ring homomorphism
   d. Square-free

7. In mathematics, especially in the area of abstract algebra known as ring theory, a _____ is a ring with 0 ≠ 1 such that ab = 0 implies that either a = 0 or b = 0 (the zero-product property.) That is, it is a nontrivial ring without left or right zero divisors. A commutative _____ is called an integral _____.
   a. Partially-ordered ring
   b. Domain
   c. Subring
   d. Coherent ring

8. In abstract algebra, a _____ is an algebraic structure with notions of addition, subtraction, multiplication and division, satisfying certain axioms. The most commonly used _____s are the _____ of real numbers, the _____ of complex numbers, and the _____ of rational numbers, but there are also finite _____s, fields of functions, various algebraic number _____s, p-adic _____s, and so forth.

Any _____ may be used as the scalars for a vector space, which is the standard general context for linear algebra.

   a. Separable
   b. Tensor product of fields
   c. Generic polynomial
   d. Field

9. In commutative algebra, the notions of an element _____ over a ring, and of an _____ extension of rings, are a generalization of the notions in field theory of an element being algebraic over a field, and of an algebraic extension of fields.

Chapter 4. Ring Theory

The special case of greatest interest in number theory is that of complex numbers _____ over the ring of integers Z.

   a. Extension and contraction of ideals
   b. Integral domain
   c. Associated prime
   d. Integral

10. In abstract algebra, an _____ is a commutative ring without zero divisors and with a multiplicative identity 1 not equal to 0, the additive identity. _____s are generalizations of the integers and provide a natural setting for studying divisibility. An _____ is a commutative domain.
   a. Invariant polynomial
   b. Atomic domain
   c. Associated prime
   d. Integral domain

11. In abstract algebra, a nonzero element a of a ring is a left _____ if there exists a nonzero b such that ab = 0. Right _____s are defined analogously, that is, a nonzero element a of a ring is a right _____ if there exists a nonzero c such that ca = 0. An element that is both a left and a right _____ is simply called a _____.
   a. Matrix
   b. Polynomial expression
   c. Zero divisor
   d. BCK algebras

12. In algebraic geometry, _____s are a generalization of codimension one subvarieties of algebraic varieties; two different generalizations are in common use, Cartier _____s and Weil _____s The concepts agree on non-singular varieties over algebraically closed fields.

A Weil _____ is a locally finite linear combination (with integral coefficients) of irreducible subvarieties of codimension one.

   a. Picard group
   b. Linear system of divisors
   c. Lefschetz pencil
   d. Divisor

13. In mathematics, a _____ is a subset of a ring, which contains the multiplicative identity and is itself a ring under the same binary operations. Naturally, those authors who do not require rings to contain a multiplicative identity do not require _____s to possess the identity (if it exists.) This leads to the added advantage that ideals become _____s
    a. Poisson ring
    b. Kurosh problem
    c. Semiperfect ring
    d. Subring

14. _____, in mathematics, are a non-commutative number system that extends the complex numbers. The _____ were first described by Irish mathematician Sir William Rowan Hamilton in 1843 and applied to mechanics in three-dimensional space. They find uses in both theoretical and applied mathematics, in particular for calculations involving three-dimensional rotations , such as in 3D computer graphics, although they have been superseded in many applications by vectors and matrices.
    a. Generalized quaternion interpolation
    b. Split-quaternions
    c. Split-biquaternion
    d. Quaternions

15. Let S be a set with a binary operation * . If e is an identity element of (S, *) and a * b = e, then a is called a _____ of b and b is called a right inverse of a. If an element x is both a _____ and a right inverse of y, then x is called a two-sided inverse, or simply an inverse, of y.
    a. Left inverse
    b. -module
    c. 2-bridge knot
    d. -equivalence

16. In mathematics, a _____ R is a ring (with identity) for which x^2 = x for all x in R; that is, R consists only of idempotent elements.

    _____s are automatically commutative and of characteristic 2 A _____ is essentially the same thing as a Boolean algebra, with ring multiplication corresponding to conjunction or meet ∧, and ring addition to exclusive disjunction or symmetric difference (not disjunction ∨.)

    a. Domain
    b. Boolean ring
    c. Hereditary
    d. Ring of integers

17. A _____ between two algebras over a field K, A and B, is a map $F : A \to B$ such that for all k in K and x,y in A,

- F(kx) = kF(x)

- F(x + y) = F(x) + F(y)

- F(xy) = F(x)F(y)

If F is bijective then F is said to be an isomorphism between A and B.

Let A = K[x] be the set of all polynomials over a field K and B be the set of all polynomial functions over K. Both A and B are algebras over K given by the standard multiplication and addition of polynomials and functions, respectively. We can map each f in A to $\hat{f}$ in B by the rule $\hat{f}(t) = f(t)$. A routine check shows that the mapping $f \mapsto \hat{f}$ is a _____ of the algebras A and B. If K is a finite field then let

$$p(x) = \Pi_{t \in K}(x - t).$$

p is a nonzero polynomial in K[x], however $p(t) = 0$ for all t in K, so $\hat{p} = 0$ is the zero function and the algebras are not isomorphic.

a. Tensor product of algebras
b. Tensor algebra
c. Frobenius matrix
d. Homomorphism

18. In ring theory, a branch of abstract algebra, an _____ is a special subset of a ring. The _____ concept generalizes in an appropriate way some important properties of integers like 'even number' or 'multiple of 3'.

For instance, in rings one studies prime _____s instead of prime numbers, one defines coprime _____s as a generalization of coprime numbers, and one can prove a generalized Chinese remainder theorem about _____s.

a. Ideal
b. ADE classification
c. Augmentation ideal
d. AKS primality test

Chapter 4. Ring Theory

19. In the various branches of mathematics that fall under the heading of abstract algebra, the _____ of a homomorphism measures the degree to which the homomorphism fails to be injective. An important special case is the _____ of a matrix, also called the null space.

The definition of _____ takes various forms in various contexts.

   a. Completing the square
   b. Monomial basis
   c. Kernel
   d. K-theory

20. In mathematics, an _____ is an isomorphism from a mathematical object to itself. It is, in some sense, a symmetry of the object, and a way of mapping the object to itself while preserving all of its structure. The set of all _____s of an object forms a group, called the _____ group.

   a. Epimorphism
   b. Endomorphism
   c. ADE classification
   d. Automorphism

21. In abstract algebra, an _____ is a bijective map f such that both f and its inverse f^{-1} are homomorphisms, i.e., structure-preserving mappings. In the more general setting of category theory, an _____ is a morphism f:X→Y in a category for which there exists an 'inverse' f^{-1}:Y→X, with the property that both $f^{-1}f = id_X$ and $ff^{-1} = id_Y$.

Informally, an _____ is a kind of mapping between objects, which shows a relationship between two properties or operations.

   a. Epimorphism
   b. Endomorphism
   c. ADE classification
   d. Isomorphism

22. In the context of abstract algebra or universal algebra, a _____ is an injective homomorphism. A _____ from X to Y is often denoted with the notation $X \hookrightarrow Y$.

In the more general setting of category theory, a _____ is a left-cancellative morphism, that is, a map f : X → Y such that, for all morphisms $g_1, g_2 : Z \to X$,

$$f \circ g_1 = f \circ g_2 \Rightarrow g_1 = g_2.$$

Chapter 4. Ring Theory

_____s are a categorical generalization of injective functions; in some categories the notions coincide, but _____s are more general, as in the examples below.

a. 2-bridge knot
b. -equivalence
c. -module
d. Monomorphism

23. In abstract algebra, the _____ is a construction which combines several modules into a new, larger module. The result of the direct summation of modules is the 'smallest general' module which contains the given modules as subspaces. This is an example of a coproduct.
a. Finite dimensional von Neumann algebra
b. Frame
c. Direct sum
d. Schmidt decomposition

24. The _____ is a result about congruences in number theory and its generalizations in abstract algebra.

The original form of the theorem, contained in a third-century AD book Sun Zi suanjing by Chinese mathematician Sun Tzu and later republished in a 1247 book by Qin Jiushao, the Shushu Jiuzhang (æ•¸æ›¸ä¹ ç« Mathematical Treatise in Nine Sections) is a statement about simultaneous congruences

Suppose n_1, n_2, â€¦, n_k are positive integers which are pairwise coprime.

a. Discrete logarithm
b. Chinese Remainder Theorem
c. Modular arithmetic
d. Multiplicative group of integers modulo n

25. In mathematics, more specifically in ring theory, a _____ is an ideal which is maximal (with respect to set inclusion) amongst all proper ideals, i.e. which is not contained in any other proper ideal of the ring.

_____s are important because the quotient rings of _____s are simple rings, and in the special case of unital commutative rings they are also fields. Rings which contain only one _____ are called local rings.

Chapter 4. Ring Theory

a. Maximal ideal
b. Radical of an ring
c. Jacobson radical
d. Principal ideal

26. In mathematics, especially in the field of abstract algebra, a _____ is a ring formed from the set of polynomials in one or more variables with coefficients in another ring. _____s have influenced much of mathematics, from the Hilbert basis theorem, to the construction of splitting fields, and to the understanding of a linear operator. Many important conjectures, such as Serre's conjecture, have influenced the study of other rings, and have influenced even the definition of other rings, such as group rings and rings of formal power series.

  a. Commutative ring
  b. Dedekind domain
  c. Nilradical
  d. Polynomial ring

27. In mathematics, a _____ is a constant multiplicative factor of a certain object. For example, in the expression $9x^2$, the _____ of x^2 is 9.

The object can be such things as a variable, a vector, a function, etc.

  a. Constant term
  b. Vandermonde polynomial
  c. Tschirnhaus transformation
  d. Coefficient

28. In mathematics, there are several meanings of _____ depending on the subject.

A _____, usually denoted by ° (the _____ symbol), is a measurement of plane angle, representing $1/360$ of a full rotation. When that angle is with respect to a reference meridian, it indicates a location along a great circle of a sphere, such as Earth, Mars, or the celestial sphere.

  a. Median algebra
  b. Symmetric difference
  c. Relation algebra
  d. Degree

Chapter 4. Ring Theory

29. In mathematics, if L is a field extension of K, then an element a of L is called an _____ over K if there exists some non-zero polynomial g(x) with coefficients in K such that g(a)=0. Elements of L which are not algebraic over K are called transcendental over K.

These notions generalize the algebraic numbers and the transcendental numbers (where the field extension is C/Q, C being the field of complex numbers and Q being the field of rational numbers.)

   a. Inverse element
   b. Indeterminate
   c. Affine Hecke algebra
   d. Algebraic element

30. In ring theory, a branch of abstract algebra, a _____ is an ideal I in a ring R that is generated by a single element a of R.

More specifically:

- a left _____ of R is a subset of R of the form Ra := {ra : r in R};
- a right _____ is a subset of the form aR := {ar : r in R};
- a two-sided _____ is a subset of the form RaR := {$r_1 a s_1$ + ... + $r_n a s_n$: $r_1, s_1, ..., r_n, s_n$ in R}.

If R is a commutative ring, then the above three notions are all the same. In that case, it is common to write the ideal generated by a as (a.)

Not all ideals are principal.

   a. Radical of an ring
   b. Radical of an ideal
   c. Primitive ideal
   d. Principal ideal

31. In abstract algebra, a _____ i.e., can be generated by a single element. More generally, a principal ring is a nonzero commutative ring whose ideals are principal, although some authors (e.g., Bourbaki) refers to _____ s as principal rings. The distinction being that a principal ideal ring may have zero divisors whereas a _____ cannot.
   a. Discrete valuation
   b. Nilradical
   c. Minimal prime
   d. Principal ideal domain

Chapter 4. Ring Theory

32. Informally, the _____ of two polynomials p(x) and q(x) is the 'biggest' polynomial that divides evenly into both p(x) and q(x.) The definition is modeled on the concept of the _____ of two integers. This is simply the greatest integer that divides into both of them with a remainder of zero.

    a. Greatest common divisor
    b. Ring of symmetric functions
    c. Coefficient
    d. Descartes' rule of signs

33. The _____ are natural numbers including 0 ' href='/wiki/0_(number)'>0, 1, 2, 3, ...) and their negatives (0, −1, −2, −3, ...). They are numbers that can be written without a fractional or decimal component, and fall within the set {...

    a. AKS primality test
    b. ADE classification
    c. Abelian P-root group
    d. Integers

34. In mathematics, the adjective _____ means that an object cannot be expressed as a product of more than one non-trivial factors in a given set. See also factorization.

For any field F, the ring of polynomials with coefficients in F is denoted by F[x].

    a. Irreducible
    b. Ehrhart polynomial
    c. Alternating polynomial
    d. Integer-valued polynomial

Chapter 5. Fields

1. In mathematics, a _____ is any function which can be written as the ratio of two polynomial functions. _____ of degree 2 : $$y = \frac{x^2 - 3x - 2}{x^2 - 4}$$

   In the case of one variable, x, a _____ is a function of the form

   $$f(x) = \frac{P(x)}{Q(x)}$$

   where P and Q are polynomial function in x and Q is not the zero polynomial. The domain of f is the set of all points x for which the denominator Q(x) is not zero.

   a. -module
   b. Rational function
   c. Legendre rational functions
   d. -equivalence

2. In mathematics, the _____ of a ring R, often denoted char(R), is defined to be the smallest number of times one must add the ring's multiplicative identity element (1) to itself to get the additive identity element (0); the ring is said to have _____ zero if this repeated sum never reaches the additive identity. That is, char(R) is the smallest positive number n such that

   $$\underbrace{1 + \cdots + 1}_{n \text{ summands}} = 0$$

   if such a number n exists, and 0 otherwise. The _____ may also be taken to be the exponent of the ring's additive group, that is, the smallest positive n such that

   $$\underbrace{a + \cdots + a}_{n \text{ summands}} = 0$$

   for every element a of the ring (again, if n exists; otherwise zero.)

   a. Hereditary
   b. Free ideal ring
   c. Characteristic
   d. Coherent ring

Chapter 5. Fields

3. In abstract algebra, a _____ is an algebraic structure with notions of addition, subtraction, multiplication and division, satisfying certain axioms. The most commonly used _____s are the _____ of real numbers, the _____ of complex numbers, and the _____ of rational numbers, but there are also finite _____s, fields of functions, various algebraic number _____s, p-adic _____s, and so forth.

Any _____ may be used as the scalars for a vector space, which is the standard general context for linear algebra.

   a. Separable
   b. Tensor product of fields
   c. Generic polynomial
   d. Field

4. In abstract algebra, the _____ is a construction which combines several modules into a new, larger module. The result of the direct summation of modules is the 'smallest general' module which contains the given modules as subspaces. This is an example of a coproduct.
   a. Frame
   b. Finite dimensional von Neumann algebra
   c. Direct sum
   d. Schmidt decomposition

5. In mathematics, a _____ is a type of algebraic structure. There is some variation among mathematicians as to exactly what properties a _____ is required to have, as described in detail below. However, commonly a _____ is defined as a set together with two binary operations (usually called addition and multiplication), where each operation combines two elements to form a third element.
   a. -module
   b. 2-bridge knot
   c. -equivalence
   d. Ring

6. In mathematics, an _____ is a statement about the relative size or order of two objects, or about whether they are the same or not

   - The notation a < b means that a is less than b.
   - The notation a > b means that a is greater than b.
   - The notation a ≠ b means that a is not equal to b, but does not say that one is bigger than the other or even that they can be compared in size.

In all these cases, a is not equal to b, hence, '_____'.

Chapter 5. Fields

These relations are known as strict _____

- The notation a ≤ b means that a is less than or equal to b (or, equivalently, not greater than b);
- The notation a ≥ b means that a is greater than or equal to b (or, equivalently, not smaller than b);

An additional use of the notation is to show that one quantity is much greater than another, normally by several orders of magnitude.

- The notation a ≪ b means that a is much less than b.
- The notation a ≫ b means that a is much greater than b.

If the sense of the _____ is the same for all values of the variables for which its members are defined, then the _____ is called an 'absolute' or 'unconditional' _____. If the sense of an _____ holds only for certain values of the variables involved, but is reversed or destroyed for other values of the variables, it is called a conditional _____.

One can apply the same algebraic operations to inequalities as one would apply for solving equalities. For example, to find x for the _____ 10x > 20 one would divide 20 by 10 to obtain x > 2.

   a. AKS primality test
   b. ADE classification
   c. Abelian P-root group
   d. Inequality

7. In mathematics, _____ are a concept central to linear algebra and related fields of mathematics

Suppose that K is a field and V is a vector space over K. As usual, we call elements of V vectors and call elements of K scalars.

   a. Left alternative
   b. Groupoid
   c. Hyperstructures
   d. Linear combinations

8. In linear algebra, a family of vectors is _____ if none of them can be written as a linear combination of finitely many other vectors in the collection. A family of vectors which is not _____ is called linearly dependent. For instance, in the three-dimensional real vector space $\mathbb{R}^3$ we have the following example.

Chapter 5. Fields

   a. Derivative algebra
   b. Composition ring
   c. Linearly independent
   d. Grothendieck group

9. A _____ is one of the basic shapes of geometry: a polygon with three corners or vertices and three sides or edges which are line segments. A _____ with vertices A, B, and C is denoted ABC.

In Euclidean geometry any three non-collinear points determine a unique _____ and a unique plane (i.e. a two-dimensional Euclidean space.)

   a. -module
   b. -equivalence
   c. 2-bridge knot
   d. Triangle

10. In mathematics, the _____ states that for any triangle, the length of a given side must be less than the sum of the other two sides but greater than the difference between the two sides.

In Euclidean geometry and some other geometries this is a theorem. In the Euclidean case, in both the less than or equal to and greater than or equal to statements, equality occurs only if the triangle has a 180° angle and two 0° angles, as shown in the bottom example in the image to the right.

   a. -equivalence
   b. -module
   c. 2-bridge knot
   d. Triangle Inequality

11. In mathematics, the _____ of a vector space V is the cardinality (i.e. the number of vectors) of a basis of V. It is sometimes called Hamel _____ or algebraic _____ to distinguish it from other types of _____. All bases of a vector space have equal cardinality and so the _____ of a vector space is uniquely defined. The _____ of the vector space V over the field F can be written as $\dim_F(V)$ or as [V : F], read '_____ of V over F'.

   a. Dimension
   b. Cofactor
   c. Partial trace
   d. Dual basis

Chapter 5. Fields

12. In linear algebra, a _____ is a set of vectors that, in a linear combination, can represent every vector in a given vector space or free module, and such that no element of the set can be represented as a linear combination of the others. In other words, a _____ is a linearly independent spanning set.

    a. Basis
    b. Supergroup
    c. Chirality
    d. Minor

13. In mathematics, there are several meanings of _____ depending on the subject.

    A _____, usually denoted by ° (the _____ symbol), is a measurement of plane angle, representing $1/360$ of a full rotation. When that angle is with respect to a reference meridian, it indicates a location along a great circle of a sphere, such as Earth, Mars, or the celestial sphere.

    a. Degree
    b. Median algebra
    c. Relation algebra
    d. Symmetric difference

14. In mathematics, more specifically in abstract algebra, _____s are the main object of study in field theory. The general idea is to start with a base field and construct in some manner a larger field which contains the base field and satisfies additional properties.

    _____s can be generalized to ring extension which consists of a ring and one of its subrings.

    a. Splitting field
    b. Real closed field
    c. Field extension
    d. Tensor product of fields

15. In mathematics, if L is a field extension of K, then an element a of L is called an _____ over K if there exists some non-zero polynomial g(x) with coefficients in K such that g(a)=0. Elements of L which are not algebraic over K are called transcendental over K.

    These notions generalize the algebraic numbers and the transcendental numbers (where the field extension is C/Q, C being the field of complex numbers and Q being the field of rational numbers.)

a. Indeterminate
b. Inverse element
c. Affine Hecke algebra
d. Algebraic element

16. In abstract algebra, a _____ or Galois field is a field that contains only finitely many elements. _____s are important in number theory, algebraic geometry, Galois theory, cryptography, and coding theory. The _____s are classified by size; there is exactly one _____ up to isomorphism of size p^k for each prime p and positive integer k.
    a. Field with one element
    b. Finite Field
    c. Frobenius endomorphism
    d. Network coding

17. In field theory, given a field extension E / F and an element α of E which is an algebraic element over F, the _____ of α is the monic polynomial p, with coefficients in F, of least degree such that p(α) = 0. The _____ is irreducible over F, and any other non-zero polynomial f with f(α) = 0 is a (polynomial) multiple of p.

    For example, for $F = \mathbb{Q}, E = \mathbb{R}, \alpha = \sqrt{2}$ the _____ for α is p(x) = x^2 − 2.
    a. Ring of symmetric functions
    b. Vandermonde polynomial
    c. Kazhdan-Lusztig polynomials
    d. Minimal polynomial

18. In mathematics, an _____ is a complex number that is a root of a non-zero polynomial in one variable with rational (or equivalently, integer) coefficients. Numbers such as pi that are not algebraic are said to be transcendental, and are infinitely more numerous within the complex number field.

- The rational numbers, those expressed as the ratio of two whole numbers b and a, a not equal to zero, satisfy the above definition because x = − b / a is derived from (and satisfies) ax + b = 0. (In general, a or b can be negative, as can x.)

- Some irrational numbers are algebraic and some are not:

    - The numbers $\sqrt{2}$ and $\sqrt[3]{3/2}$ are algebraic since they are the roots of $x^2 - 2 = 0$ and $8x^3 - 3 = 0$, respectively.

    - The golden ratio φ is algebraic since it is a root of the polynomial $x^2 - x - 1 = 0$.

    - The numbers π and e are not _____s ; hence they are transcendental.

- The constructible numbers (those that, starting with a unit, can be constructed with straightedge and compass, e.g. the square root of 2) are algebraic.

- The quadratic surds (roots of a quadratic equation $ax^2 + bx + c = 0$ with integer coefficients a, b, and c) are _____s. Thus those complex numbers derived from $ax^2 + bx + c = 0$ -- those corresponding to the case when the exponent n = 2 -- are called quadratic numbers.

a. External
b. Universal algebra
c. Algebraic number
d. Unit ring

19. In mathematics, a field F is said to be _____ if every polynomial in one variable of degree at least 1, with coefficients in F, has a root in F.

As an example, the field of real numbers is not _____, because the polynomial equation $x^2 + 1 = 0$ has no solution in real numbers, even though all its coefficients (1 and 0) are real. The same argument proves that no subfield of the real field is _____; in particular, the field of rational numbers is not _____.

a. Ordered exponential
b. Algebraically closed
c. Unique factorization domain
d. Inverse semigroup

Chapter 5. Fields

20. In geometry and trigonometry, an _____ is the figure formed by two rays sharing a common endpoint, called the vertex of the _____ . The magnitude of the _____ is the 'amount of rotation' that separates the two rays, and can be measured by considering the length of circular arc swept out when one ray is rotated about the vertex to coincide with the other Where there is no possibility of confusion, the term '_____' is used interchangeably for both the geometric configuration itself and for its angular magnitude (which is simply a numerical quantity.)
    a. Angle
    b. ADE classification
    c. Abelian P-root group
    d. AKS primality test

21. A _____ is a three-dimensional solid object bounded by six square faces, facets or sides, with three meeting at each vertex. The _____ can also be called a regular hexahedron and is one of the five Platonic solids. It is a special kind of square prism, of rectangular parallelepiped and of trigonal trapezohedron.
    a. 2-bridge knot
    b. -module
    c. Cube
    d. -equivalence

22. In abstract algebra, the _____ of a module is a measure of the module's 'size'. It is defined as the _____ of the longest ascending chain of submodules and is a generalization of the concept of dimension for vector spaces. The modules with finite _____ share many important properties with finite-dimensional vector spaces.
    a. Morita equivalence
    b. Supermodule
    c. Length
    d. Finitely generated module

23. In mathematics, a _____ of a number x is any number which, when repeatedly multiplied by itself, eventually yields x:

$$r \times r \times \cdots \times r = x.$$

In terms of exponentiation, r is a _____ of x if

$$r^n = x$$

for some positive integer n. For example, 2 is a _____ of 16 since $2^4 = 2 \times 2 \times 2 \times 2 = 16$.

The number n is called the degree of the _____.

Chapter 5. Fields

   a. Cubic function
   b. Rationalisation
   c. Difference of two squares
   d. Root

24. In mathematics, more specifically in abstract algebra, _____ provides a connection between field theory and group theory. Using _____, certain problems in field theory can be reduced to group theory, which is in some sense simpler and better understood.

Originally Galois used permutation groups to describe how the various roots of a given polynomial equation are related to each other.

   a. Simple extension
   b. Galois theory
   c. Separable
   d. Galois group

25. In abstract algebra, the _____ of a polynomial P(X) over a given field K is a field extension L of K, over which P factorizes into linear factors

   $X - a_i$,

and such that the a_i generate L over K. It can be shown that such _____s exist, and are unique up to isomorphism; the amount of freedom in that isomorphism is known to be the Galois group of P.

For an example if K is the rational number field Q and

   $P = X^3 - 2$,

then a _____ L will contain a primitive cube root of unity, as well as a cube root of 2. Thus

$$L = \mathbb{Q}(\sqrt[3]{2}, \omega_2) = \{a + b\omega_2 + c\sqrt[3]{2} + d\sqrt[3]{2}\omega_2 + e\sqrt[3]{2}^2 + f\sqrt[3]{2}^2\omega_2 \mid a, b, c, d, e, f \in \mathbb{Q}\}$$

where

$$\omega_1 = 1,$$
$$\omega_2 = -\frac{1}{2} + \frac{\sqrt{3}}{2}i, \text{ and}$$
$$\omega_3 = -\frac{1}{2} - \frac{\sqrt{3}}{2}i$$

are the cubic roots of unity.

a. Formally real field
b. Fundamental theorem of Galois theory
c. Field of fractions
d. Splitting field

Chapter 6. Special Topics (Optional)   43

1. In mathematics, an _____ is the group of even permutations of a finite set. The _____ on the set {1,...,n} is called the _____ of degree n, or the _____ on n letters and denoted by A_n or Alt(n.)

For instance, the _____ of degree 4 is A_4 = {e, (123), (132), (124), (142), (134), (143), (234), (243), (12)(34), (13)(24), (14)(23)}

   a. Alternating group
   b. Icosahedral symmetry
   c. Extra special groups
   d. Octahedral symmetry

2. A _____ is a set G closed under a binary operation · satisfying the following 3 axioms:

   - Associativity: For all a, b and c in G, (a · b) · c = a · (b · c.)
   - Identity element: There exists an e∈G such that for all a in G, e · a = a · e = a.
   - Inverse element: For each a in G, there is an element b in G such that a · b = b · a = e, where e is an identity element.

Basic examples for _____s are the integers Z with addition operation, or rational numbers without zero Q{0} with multiplication. More generally, for any ring R, the units in R form a multiplicative _____ Groups include, however, much more general structures than the above.

   a. Grigorchuk group
   b. Group
   c. Nilpotent group
   d. Product of group subsets

3. In mathematics, the term _____ is used to describe an algebraic structures which in some sense cannot be divided by a smaller structure of the same type. Put another way, an algebraic structure is _____ if the kernel of every homomorphism is either the whole structure or a single element. Some examples are:

   - A group is called a _____ group if it does not contain a non-trivial proper normal subgroup.
   - A ring is called a _____ ring if it does not contain a non-trivial two sided ideal.
   - A module is called a _____ module if does not contain a non-trivial submodule.
   - An algebra is called a _____ algebra if does not contain a non-trivial two sided ideal.

The general pattern is that the structure admits no non-trivial congruence relations.

a. Polarization identity
b. Commutativity
c. Linear combinations
d. Simple

4. In mathematics, the _____ is an operation on elements of a polynomial ring or a ring of formal power series which mimics the form of the derivative from calculus. Though they appear similar, the algebraic advantage of a _____ is that it does not rely on the notion of a limit, which is in general impossible to define for a ring. Many of the properties of the derivative are true of the _____, but some, especially those which make numerical statements, are not.
a. Composition ring
b. Formal derivative
c. Power set
d. Fundamental theorem on homomorphisms

5. The _____ is often met for the first time as an operation on a single real function of a single real variable. One of the simplest settings for generalizations is to vector valued functions of several variables (most often the domain forms a vector space as well.) This is the field of multivariable calculus.
a. -module
b. Derivative
c. 2-bridge knot
d. -equivalence

6. In mathematics, a _____ of a number x is any number which, when repeatedly multiplied by itself, eventually yields x:

$$r \times r \times \cdots \times r = x.$$

In terms of exponentiation, r is a _____ of x if

$$r^n = x$$

for some positive integer n. For example, 2 is a _____ of 16 since $2^4 = 2 \times 2 \times 2 \times 2 = 16$.

The number n is called the degree of the _____.

a. Cubic function
b. Root
c. Rationalisation
d. Difference of two squares

7. An nth _____, where n = 1,2,3,··· , is a complex number, z, satisfying the equation

$$z^n = 1.$$

Second roots are called square roots, and third roots are called cube roots.

An nth _____ is primitive if

$$z^k \neq 1 \quad (k = 1, 2, 3, \ldots, n-1).$$

There are n different nth roots of unity:

$$z^k \quad (k = 1, 2, 3, \ldots, n),$$

where z is any primitive nth _____. These n roots are distributed evenly over the unit circle as can be seen in the plot on the right-hand side of the three 3rd roots of unity.

a. -module
b. 2-bridge knot
c. -equivalence
d. Root of unity

8. In algebra, the nth _____, for any positive integer n, is the monic polynomial

where the product is over all primitive nth roots of unity ω, i.e. all the complex numbers ω of order n.

The degree of Φ_n, or in other words the number of factors in its definition above, is φ(n), where φ is Euler's totient function.

The coefficients of Φ_n are integers.

a. Cyclic number
b. Character group
c. Cyclotomic polynomial
d. Q-Vandermonde identity

ANSWER KEY

Chapter 1
1. d 2. d 3. d 4. b 5. c 6. d 7. d 8. a 9. c 10. d
11. d 12. b 13. c 14. d 15. c 16. c 17. d 18. d 19. d 20. c
21. d 22. b

Chapter 2
1. d 2. d 3. a 4. d 5. a 6. d 7. d 8. d 9. a 10. b
11. d 12. c 13. d 14. d 15. d 16. d 17. d 18. c 19. a 20. d
21. d 22. b 23. d 24. b 25. d

Chapter 3
1. b 2. d 3. a 4. a 5. d

Chapter 4
1. b 2. c 3. d 4. d 5. b 6. a 7. b 8. d 9. d 10. d
11. c 12. d 13. d 14. d 15. a 16. b 17. d 18. a 19. c 20. d
21. d 22. d 23. c 24. b 25. a 26. d 27. d 28. d 29. d 30. d
31. d 32. a 33. d 34. a

Chapter 5
1. b 2. c 3. d 4. c 5. d 6. d 7. d 8. c 9. d 10. d
11. a 12. a 13. a 14. c 15. d 16. b 17. d 18. c 19. b 20. a
21. c 22. c 23. d 24. b 25. d

Chapter 6
1. a 2. b 3. d 4. b 5. b 6. b 7. d 8. c